101 CANADIAN JOKES

Howard Hershkowitz

Illustrated by
Bill Dickson

Scholastic Canada Ltd.

Toronto New York London Auckland Sydney
Mexico City New Delhi Hong Kong Buenos Aires

Scholastic Canada Ltd.
604 King Street West, Toronto, Ontario M5V 1E1, Canada

Scholastic Inc.
557 Broadway, New York, NY 10012, USA

Scholastic Australia Pty Limited
PO Box 579, Gosford, NSW 2250, Australia

Scholastic New Zealand Limited
Private Bag 94407, Botany, Manukau 2163, New Zealand

Scholastic Children's Books
Euston House, 24 Eversholt Street
London NW1 1DB, UK

National Library of Canada Cataloguing in Publication

Hershkowitz, Howard
101 Canadian jokes / Howard Hershkowitz ; illustrated by Bill Dickson.

ISBN 0-439-96108-4

1. Canadian wit and humor (English) I. Dickson, Bill II. Title. III.
Title: One hundred and one Canadian jokes.

PS8375.H47 2004   jC817'.608   C2004-901791-8
ISBN-13:978-0-439-96108-4

Oh Canada!

If you're Canadian in the kitchen, what are you in the bathroom?

European.

What did the Canadian flag say to the pole?

Nothing, it just waved.

Did you hear the one about the cottager who lit a fire in her boat and had to swim ashore when it sank?

It just goes to show, you can't have your kayak and heat it too!

Why did the rancher ride
his horse?

Because the horse was too heavy
to carry.

What did the man say when his
neighbour finished building
his igloo?

"That's an ice house you have there!"

If a man was born in France, then
raised in England, moved to Canada
and died in Quebec, what is he?

Dead.

What does Canada produce that no other country produces?

Canadians.

How do you spell Canada?

C, eh? N, eh? D, eh?

If a plane crashes on the U.S./Canada border, where does the law require the survivors to be buried?

Nowhere, silly — you don't bury the survivors!

Attention Sports Fans

What sort of ball doesn't bounce?

A snowball.

How do you keep bacon from curling in the pan?

Take away their little brooms.

How do you kiss a hockey player?

Puck-er up . . .

Skating coach: *Did anyone laugh when you fell down?*

Skater: *No, but the ice made some awful cracks.*

How does Wayne Gretzky
stay cool?

He sits next to his fans.

What is the messiest sport played in Canada?

Basketball, because the players dribble on the floor.

What do a hockey player and a magician have in common?

Both do hat tricks!

Why did the Canada goose run
onto the soccer field?

Because the referee called a foul.

What goes all around a hockey rink
but never moves?

The boards.

What is the hardest part about skating?

The ice — when you get right down to it!

Why did the boy climb up a tree with his hockey stick?

Because he wanted to play with the Maple Leafs.

Animal Country

Why do seagulls live near the sea?

If they lived near the bay, they'd be bagels.

Why did the otter cross the road?

To get to the otter side.

Why did the duck cross the road?

Because the chicken retired and moved to Florida.

How do you get milk from a polar bear?

Raid its fridge and run like mad.

Why did the buffalo cross the road?

It was the chicken's day off.

Why did the lobster cross the road?

To get to the other tide.

What do you get when you cross
a groundhog with a Maple Leaf?

Six more weeks of hockey.

What is big and white and found
in Vancouver?

A lost polar bear.

What has one hump, is brown and
wanders Nunavut?

A lost camel.

What is the difference between a beaver and a chain saw?

Eighty trees an hour.

How do you keep a grizzly bear from charging?

Take away its credit cards.

What do you call a polar bear with no socks on?

Bear-foot.

What did the Canada goose say
when she saw a plate of
scrambled eggs?

*"What a bunch of crazy, mixed-up
kids!"*

Who does a dog quarterback
throw to?

A Labrador receiver.

What do you call a dog that sits in a snowdrift?

A chili dog!

Where does a 300-kilo grizzly bear sit?

Anywhere it wants.

What kind of pine has the sharpest needles?

The porcupine.

What did the beaver say to the maple tree?

"It's been nice gnawing you."

What do you call a herd of giggling cattle?

Laughingstock.

Where do sled drivers keep dog food?

In the mushroom.

How do you catch a squirrel?

Climb a tree and act like a nut!

Why did the rancher take his cow
to the vet?

Because she was moooody.

What is the Canada goose's favourite
TV show?

The feather report.

What bird gasps and pants on Newfoundland's coast?

A puffin.

What kind of bears like to go out in the rain?

Drizzly bears.

Why do polar bears wear fur coats?

Because they would look silly in ski jackets.

What Really Bugs Us

What is a mosquito's favourite sport?

Skin-diving.

What has six legs, bites and talks in code?

A morse-quito.

How do you know if you have a tough mosquito?

You slap him and he slaps you back.

What has antlers and sucks blood?

A moose-quito.

Why did the mosquito go to the dentist?

To improve his bite.

What insects love math class?

Mosquitoes — they add to misery, subtract from pleasure, divide your attention and multiply quickly.

Snow Much Fun

What do snowmen wear on their heads?

Ice caps.

What happened when the snowgirl broke up with the snowboy?

She gave him the cold shoulder.

Where do snowmen go to dance?

Snowballs.

How do snowmen make their beds?

With sheets of ice and blankets of snow.

What do snowmen eat for lunch?

Icebergers.

How do snowmen travel around?

By icicle.

What do you get if you cross a
snowman and a shark?

Frost bite.

What two letters of the alphabet do snowmen prefer?

I.C.

Where do snowmen keep their money?

In a snow bank.

Somewhere in Canada

Did you hear about the guy who just flew in from St. John's?

Boy, were his arms tired!

If a toonie and a loonie were on the Calgary Tower, which would jump off first?

The loonie, because it has less cents.

Where do polar bears vote?

The North poll.

What's in the middle of Alberta?

The letter E.

Sean: *Where were you born?*

Greg: *Nova Scotia.*

Sean: *What part?*

Greg: *All of me!*

What do you get when you put a chicken on top of the CN Tower?

Beacon and eggs.

What's the scariest lake in Canada?

Lake Erie.

What's the best lake in Canada?

Lake Superior.

Jane: *So, have you lived in British Columbia all your life?*

Sue: *Not yet.*

George: *Come on, Sam, hurry up!*

Sam: *I'm rushin', I'm rushin'!*

George: *That's funny, I thought you were Canadian!*

What is the Yukoner's favourite song?

Freeze a jolly good fellow.

Weather Report

What is ploughed but never planted?

Snow.

Curtis: *Great news, the teacher says we have a test today come rain or shine.*

Paul: *So what's so great about that?*

Curtis: *It's snowing!*

What happened when the icicle
landed on the girl's head?

It knocked her cold!

When is a canoe like a heap of
snow?

When it's adrift.

What did the man put on his car
when the weather was cold?

An extra muffler.

What would you do if the country
was flooded?

Drink Canada Dry!

How many seasons does Canada have?

*Two — six months of winter and
six months of poor snowmobiling.*

Why do skeletons hate winter?

Because the wind goes right through them.

How do you make antifreeze?

Take away her housecoat.

Why is snow easier to understand than any other weather?

Because you can catch the drift.

Time for School

Teacher: *How did the Vikings send secret messages?*

Student: *By Norse code.*

Mother: *Why aren't you doing very well in Canadian history?*

Kid: *Because the teacher keeps asking about things that happened before I was born!*

Teacher: *Why did the voyageurs cross the country in canoes?*

Student: *Because they didn't want to wait 150 years for a train.*

Teacher: *Where was the British North America Act signed?*

Student: *At the bottom.*

Teacher: *Name the first settler in the West.*

Student: *The Sun!*

What's the smartest province?

Newfoundland and Labrador, because it has four As and a B!

Amanda: *How many feet does a moose have?*

Paul: *Six — forelegs at the front, and two at the back.*

Teacher: *How do you spell Saskatchewan?*

Student: *The province or the river?*

Teacher: *Who succeeded Canada's first prime minister?*

Student: *The second one!*

Student: *My teacher was mad at me because I don't know where the Rockies are.*

Mother: *Well, next time remember where you put things!*

Teacher: Why do birds fly south for the winter?

Student: Because it's too far to walk.

Hey, Mom! There's a Canadian at the Door!

Knock, knock!
Who's there?
Canoe.
Canoe who?
Canoe tell me some knock-knock jokes?

Knock, knock!
Who's there?
Toboggan.
Toboggan who?
I like toboggan with salespeople.

Knock, knock!
Who's there?
Gander.
Gander who?
I be-gander worry you wouldn't ask!

Knock, knock!
Who's there?
Huron.
Huron who?
Huron my foot!

Knock, knock!
Who's there?
Terrace.
Terrace who?
Terrace no place like BC!

Knock, knock!
Who's there?
Snow.
Snow who?
Snowbody but me!

Knock, knock!
Who's there?
Amos.
Amos who?
Amosquito just bit me.

ock, knock!
o's there?
ndy.
Andy who?
Andy just bit me again!